Come to Egypt!

By Clem King

Come to Egypt!

Egypt is a place in the north of Africa.

There is so much to see!

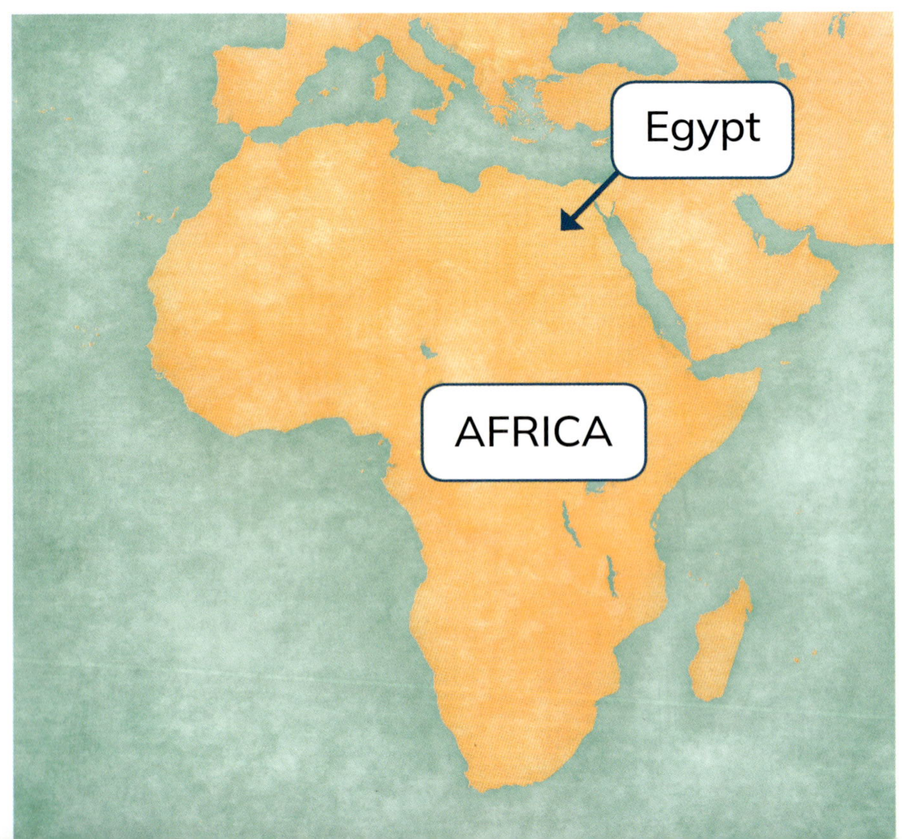

When you come to Egypt,
you will fly into a fun
and busy city.

From the sky,
you can see lots of old buildings.

Egypt is a very hot, dry place.

It has lots of huge sand dunes.

You can ride this lumpy animal across the sand!

It's not a yak.
It's a camel!

Camels can go a very long way without a drink of water.

You can ride a camel
to this pyramid.

A pyramid is a giant building
with a pointy top.
The sides of the pyramid slope up
to the top.

Why did people build pyramids?

A pyramid is a crypt for a king from long, long ago.

A crypt is like a grave.

A king's body is inside this case.

The body is called a mummy.

Away from the city,
you can visit some rocky canyons.

This is White Canyon.

This is Red Canyon.

It's very dusty!

Back in the busy city, you can try a kebab from this shop.

Then you should try these dumplings with sticky syrup.

You would be lucky to visit Egypt.

See the pyramids!

Visit the canyons!

And eat some syrupy dumplings!

CHECKING FOR MEANING

1. How does the author describe camels in the text? *(Literal)*
2. What is Red Canyon like? *(Literal)*
3. Why do you think the author says that you would be lucky to visit Egypt? *(Inferential)*
4. Do you think you would enjoy visiting Egypt? Why? *(Evaluative)*

EXTENDING VOCABULARY

lumpy	What does something look like if it is lumpy? What word means the opposite of *lumpy*?
crypt	What is a crypt? Where else might a person's body be buried?
syrup	What are the sounds in the word *syrup*? What is syrup? What might you put syrup on?

MOVING BEYOND THE TEXT

1. What would you most like to see or do in Egypt? Why?
2. Have you ever tried the Egyptian foods featured in the text? Would you like to? Why?
3. If you could travel to any country, where would you go? Why?
4. What other places do you know where you can see lots of sand?

TIME TO WRITE

Write about a place you would like to visit. What can you do there? What can you see there?